essentials

Help Your 5–7 Year Old Read Well

Parents' essentials – friendly books for busy parents
to help their children fulfil their potential.

For full details please send for a free copy of the latest catalogue.
See back cover for address.

Help Your 5–7 Year Old Read Well

Ken Adams

PARENTS' ESSENTIALS

Published in 2001 by
How To Books Ltd, 3 Newtec Place,
Magdalen Road, Oxford OX4 1RE, United Kingdom
Tel: (01865) 793806   Fax: (01865) 248780
email: info@howtobooks.co.uk
www.howtobooks.co.uk

British Library Cataloguing in Publication Data.
A catalogue record for this book is available from
the British Library.

Cover design by Shireen Nathoo Design
Produced for How To Books by Deer Park Productions
Typeset by PDQ Typesetting, Newcastle-under-Lyme, Staffordshire
Printed and bound in Great Britain by The Baskerville Press Ltd.

NOTE: The material contained in this book is set out in good faith
for general guidance and no liability can be accepted for loss or
expense incurred as a result of relying in particular circumstances
on statements made in the book. Laws and regulations are complex
and liable to change, and readers should check the current position
with the relevant authorities before making personal arrangements.

ESSENTIALS *is an imprint of*
How To Books

Contents

Preface

In recent years there has been a great increase of parental involvement in their children's reading, and help with early schoolwork. Parents buy reading and picture books, work books and CD Roms, so that their child will reap the benefits of being able to read well by an early age.

Such help ensures that not only areas of English will improve, but also the understanding of science and maths. A good basis of reading at 5–7 years old is the bedrock on which most schoolwork is built, and will ensure success in testing at all stages of learning.

This book aims to show parents how to help their child to progress his or her early reading from basic skills to being a competent reader. It follows a structured and step-wise system using phonics as a basis. There are extensive reading and practice examples within the book, much of it original material which has been created specifically to give enjoyment as well as to make the development of reading fast and easy.

Through such a system, your child will fulfil his or her potential in the area of reading, and also in every other aspect of schoolwork.

Ken Adams

1 Learning in Steps

This book aims to help you guide your child through learning reading skills, from phonics to more complicated patterns. This is achieved by a series of steps that build one on the other, and uses games, puzzles and other techniques to develop your child's memorisation of reading patterns. It aims to move from the simple to the complex, from the use of real-life aids to the recognition of more abstract symbols. Many words can be easily related to concrete objects, for example – cat, dog, moon, blot. Other words are best learnt by pattern recognition – who?, why?, what? – and by building into simple sentences. This is because for many words no clear mental image comes readily to mind for a 5 or 6-year-old child. Words like 'the' or 'here' are often learnt from the context of a sentence:

'the boy is in the garden.'

'The' (definite) boy is in 'the' (definite) garden, as opposed to 'a' boy and 'a' garden. Similarly, '*here* is the boy', has the opposite meaning to '*there* is the boy'.

These subtleties are difficult to explain to a small child, but are best learnt in context, because it is impossible to avoid such words in even simple reading texts.

STEP-WISE LEARNING

To ensure fast and effective learning, reading skills are best learnt by moving through closely related steps from the simple to the complex.

As a starting point, **phonics** forms a good base on which to build more complex reading matter. The phonic alphabet represents the single most important basis for this:

'a' for apple

'b' for boot, etc.

In particular, the starting letters of words are best learnt through the phonic alphabet; and when these are ingrained in the reader's thinking, simple phonic words can be built from them:

c – a – t

b – a – t

c – o – t

Later, these words become part of more complex words – *cat*apult, *cat*erpillar, *bat*tle, *cot*tage, S*cot*, etc.

Working in this way, the general trend is from the simple to the more complex through step-wise learning that makes new learning something that closely matches what is known already.

FROM REAL LIFE TO ABSTRACT

Tied in with the overall movement from the simple to the complex is the gradual move from real-life learning with concrete objects, to the use of abstract symbols. Since most of a young child's understanding is through an experience of the real world, then it is logical to take this as a basis for building new experiences in reading, which are essential abstract. By five years of age, for example, your child has a good knowledge of real-life objects in their environment, is often aware of their functions (a chair is for sitting), and can attach a **spoken** word to the object. They will also be able to use spoken action words like walk, run, jump, etc. Most children of this age have a good knowledge of colloquialisms like 'be quiet' or 'stop that'. Word knowledge of the spoken variety is, in fact, quite extensive. Also, there will be knowledge of written letters and words – perhaps the alphabet and simple words like 'shop', 'road', etc. It is on this base of real-life knowledge that all other, more abstract, knowledge will be built.

MOTIVATION AND CONCENTRATION

Even when methods are in place that can ensure fast and efficient learning skills, a child still needs to enjoy and feel the drive to learn. Reading material needs to be relevant to your child's interests, otherwise they will tend to watch TV, play computer games, or football, rather than become interested in words on the page. This can be achieved by the use of rhyme and rhythm, through interesting characters, pictures and stories.

At a very young age, colourful and interesting pictures that tell the story and show the characters are almost essential, although you can also play a part in acting out what happens.

Phonic Beginnings

WHAT YOUR CHILD KNOWS

Your child at age five may be anything from a total non-reader to a very good reader indeed. These are extremes, though. In between, the vast majority will know some words, picked up from signs, from around the house, from books, from computer games, and they may know some or all of the alphabet. This may not be knowledge of letters with phonic sounds:

a is for apple, etc.

Try them with these sounds first:

a for apple
b for bat
c for cat
d for dog
e for egg
f for fox
g for gate
h for hat
i for insect
j for jam
k for kite
l for ladder
m for man
n for nut
o for orange
p for pot
q for queen
r for rabbit

s for sun

t for tap

u for umbrella

v for van

w for watch

x as in bo**x**

y for yacht

z for zebra

All the words associated with the letters represent real-life objects, and are often recognised in text after learning this type of alphabet.

Phonic words

These include three-letter words with phonic letters:

cat, dog, sun, tap, hot, etc.

If your child is not yet reading such simple words, then this will be the place to start reading work.

Try these

You will first need to find out what your child knows. A good starting point will be to determine if they know the following words:

bus	cat	cup	dad
dog	egg	fox	hot
jug	man	mug	mum

pen	pin	red	sun
top	van	a	it
is	in	on	not

These are phonic words. Any difficulty will indicate a weakness in phonics. Other words that he or she may recognise are:

shop	book	car	
the	and	his	her
she	he		

Your child may well recognise other words, and miss some of those just mentioned. The final judgement on what they know has to be up to you.

A PHONIC ADVENTURE

A story and rhyme form as shown below should help to improve your child's ability with phonics.

Dib and Dab

Dib, Dab, Dob and Baby Glub are bugs who live in the middle of a wood. King of the wood is Slug, who has the giant bug, Bug, to help him. Slug is bad.

Dob likes the King. Dob wants presents, so he robs the shop in the middle of the town for the King. Then the cop comes after him, to put him in the Jug. All the people in the wood stand up for Dob. They are Cat, Spoon, Bun, Sun and Moon. So, Dob is saved, and all the people dance around the big tree.

Dib, Dab, Dob, Dob

1. Dib, Dab
   Dob, Dob.
   Slug, Slug,
   Bug, Bug.
   They all live together
   In the middle of a wood.
   Glub, Glub,
   Blob, Blob,
   In a tree,
   In a tree.
   With a bee,
   Buzz, buzz.

Tree, tree

Bug, bug

Dib, dib

Baby glub,
glub, glub

Slug, slug

Moon, moon

Spoon, spoon

Cat, cat

Dab, dab

Dob, dob

Sun, sun

Bun, bun

Jug, jug

2. Dib, Dab,
   Dob, Dob,
   Sit down,
   Sit down.
   In the middle of the town.
   Clap hands,
   Clap hands,
   Stamp feet,
   Stamp feet.
   Get the seat,
   To the seat,
   To the seat,
   In the middle of the street.

3. Glub, glub
   Rub, rub
   In the middle of the tub.
   Tub, tub,
   Rub, rub,
   Swish, swish
   Swish, swish.
   Like a fish,
   Fish, fish.
   On a dish,
   Dish, dish.

Glub, glub,
Glub, glub,
In the middle of the tub.

4. He's the slug,
   Slug, slug.
   A bad, bad lad,
   Sad, sad, lad, lad.
   He's the King,
   King, King.
   Let everybody sing,
   To the King, King, King.
   Bring presents to the King.

5. It's the bug, bug, bug.
   He's big, big, big.
   With a wig, wig, wig.
   Pal, pal to the King.
   To the King, King, King.
   For the slug, slug, slug.

6. Dob, dob.
   Bad boy,
   Wants a little toy,
   From the King, King, King.
   Dob, dob,
   Toy, toy,
   Bad boy, bad boy.

7. In the wood,
   In the wood,
   Be good, be good.
   Sit on the mat
   Like a big, fat cat,
   Cat, cat, fat, fat.
   Tap, tap,
   Tap, tap,
   Dob, Dob,
   Sob, sob.
   Who are you going to rob?
   Dob, Dob,
   At the shop,
   At the top.
   Call a cop,
   Call a cop.
   Turn the tap,
   Turn the tap.
   Tap, tap,
   Rap, rap.
   Knock at the door.
   Fall on the floor.
   Slap, slap.
   Tap, tap,
   Snap, snap.

8. Slug, slug,
   Bug, bug.
   Put them in the jug,
   Jug, jug, jug, jug.
   With a mug,
   With a mug,
   Mug, mug.
   Dob, dob,
   Bad boy,
   Let him go,
   Bad boy, bad boy,
   No toy, no toy.

3 Blends and Magic 'e'

DOUBLE BLENDS

In Chapter 2, many of the words had double blends or combinations:

glub, swish, fish, slug, King,
br ing, wood, knock, slap, snap,
stamp, str eet, clap, tr ee,
sing, sp oon, moon, feet.

A fuller list of these words useful for progressing a 5–7-year-old's reading includes:

ant	clip	flock	moon	sting
blot	clap	flick	nest	stung
blub	clop	frock	pram	stop
blue	cluck	food	queen	street
black	crisp	fish	ring	trap
blob	crack	glub	rang	treat
boot	crab	glob	rung	trip
brick	crust	green	ship	this
bring	creep	grip	shop	that
chat	drop	grub	slug	there
chin	drip	ink	stamp	twin
cheep	dish	jump	sang	vest
chop	desk	jack	sing	west
cheer	disk	lamp	sung	wing
chip	feet	lost	spot	wood
chick	foot	long	spoon	

Try these

Get your child to join word to picture.

boot

crab

foot

fish

frock

lamp

moon

ring

ship

spot

spoon

stamp

vest

wing

tree

Get your child to rearrange these jumbled words and fit them with the correct picture:

teef

shfi

noom

ngir

pish

reet

inwg

ckofr

ampl

Try this crossword

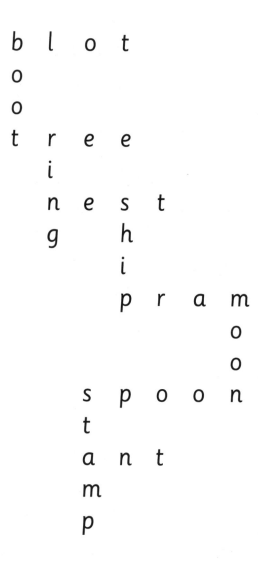

MAGIC 'E'

Phonic words e.g. (h – a – t) have short vowels ('a' for apple, etc.), and sometimes adding an 'e' to the end of such a word changes it to a long vowel (h **a** t – h **a** t e). Examples of such magical transformations are:

bit	–	bit**e**
can	–	can**e**
cap	–	cap**e**
cod	–	cod**e**
din	–	din**e**
fin	–	fin**e**
hat	–	hat**e**
kit	–	kit**e**
man	–	man**e**
pan	–	pan**e**
pin	–	pin**e**
rip	–	rip**e**
tap	–	tap**e**
win	–	win**e**

For helping your child to understand these changes, words representing real-life objects are best. Unfortunately, many words produced by adding magic 'e' are abstract (e.g. mop – mope).

Try these

Add an 'e' to make the name of the pictures, and join the words to the correct pictures.

Add 'e'

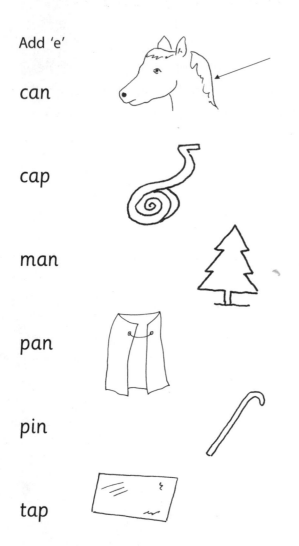

can

cap

man

pan

pin

tap

These are a little harder than earlier examples, so be especially patient if your child struggles a little.

4 Using Simple Rhymes and Stories

Nursery rhymes are often the perfect material to expand your child's reading from purely phonic work into more general reading. They are probably well acquainted with many rhymes, and this lends interest to learning to read them.

Polly put the kettle on,
Polly put the kettle on,
Polly put the kettle on,
We'll all have tea.

Sukey take it off again,
Sukey take it off again,
Sukey take it off again,
They've all gone away.

The repetition and simple wording is easily picked up by most children, and these words are learnt quickly. You may need to explain to your child what is happening here, although they may quickly get the gist. With nursery rhymes the rhythm and rhyme are an excellent aid to memorising, particularly as your child's interest is aroused.

Many rhymes have a mixture of simple words and more difficult ones. The following rhymes have been picked for this section, because they have a good share of easily learnt words and phrases. Some words you will need to explain to your child.

Jack and Jill
Went up the hill
To fetch a pail of water.
Jack fell down,
And broke his crown,
And Jill came tumbling after.

Two little birds sat
On a wall,
One named Peter,
One named Paul.
Fly away Peter
Fly away Paul
Come back Peter
Come back Paul.

Humpty Dumpty,
Sat on a wall.
Humpty Dumpty,
Had a great fall.
All the King's horses,
All the King's men,
Couldn't put Humpty together again.

Mary had a little lamb
Its fleece was white as snow,
And everywhere that Mary went,
The lamb was sure to go.

This rhyme introduces silent letters – 'lam**b**' and 'w**h**ite', and 'fleece', 'everywhere' and 'sure' are difficult words for some early readers.

Hickory, Dickory, Dock,
The mouse ran up the clock.
The clock struck one,
The mouse ran down,
Hickory, Dickory, Dock.

'Mouse' is usually the difficult word here.

Hey diddle diddle,
The cat and the fiddle,
The cow jumped over the moon.
The little dog laughed to see such fun,
And the dish ran away with the spoon.

'Laughed' is the only really difficult word here. For a small child it is puzzlingly far from phonic constructions.

Baa, baa black sheep,
Have you any wool?
Yes, sir; yes, sir,
Three bags full.
One for the master,
One for the dame,
And one for the little boy,
Who lives down the lane.

Then there is this delicious offering:

Dance to your daddy,
My little laddie,
Dance to your daddy,
My little lamb.
You shall have a fishy,
On a little dishie.
You shall have a fishy,
When the boat comes in.

Improving further reading is by extending into story rhymes and short stories. Both need to be well illustrated to stimulate your child's interest. Some picture book stories are very useful for extending reading, if the level of reading has been well thought out.

Teddy Bear's Playtime

1. Monday morning, Postman Ted;
   Sort the letters, post the mail,
   Envelopes and stamps for sale.
   Count the parcels up to ten,
   Then we play this game again.
   When it's dark you go away,
   To come and play another day.

2. Tuesday morning, Busman Ted;
   Board the bus and climb the stairs.
   Ding the bell, collect the fares.
   Count the bus stops up to ten
   Then we play this game again.
   When it's dark you go away
   To come and play another day.

3. Wednesday morning, Shopman Ted;
   Stack the tins and ring the till,
   Give the customer his bill.
   Count the money up to ten
   Then we play this game again.
   When it's dark you go away
   To come and play another day.

4. Thursday morning, Trainman Ted;
   Fill the train from front to back,
   Blow the whistle round the track.
   Count the stations up to ten
   Then we play this game again.
   When it's dark you go away
   To come and play another day.

5. Friday morning, Policemen Ted;
   Guide the traffic, walk the beat,
   Guard the bank that's in High Street.

Count the robbers up to ten
Then we play this game again.
When it's dark you go away
To come and play another day.

6. Saturday morning, Doctor Ted;
Give the pills for coughs and
   sneezes,
Bandage bones and cure diseases.
Count the patients up to ten
Then we play this game again.
When it's dark you go away
To come and play another day.

7. Sunday morning, rest-day Ted;
Put our feet up, watch TV,
Read the papers, have some tea.
Count our fingers up to ten
Till we play this game again.
When it's dark this time you'll stay,
Tomorrow is another day.

(Ken Adams)

The repetition of the last three lines aids memorisation of
words like 'dark', 'away', 'morning', 'come' and 'again'. Words
are phrases mentioned only once that are sometimes difficult,
include: days of the week, envelopes, parcels, another, board,

climb, collect, count, customer, whistle, stations, traffic, high, coughs, bandage, diseases, patients.

The poem reinforces many phonic word structures, and helps to teach the days of the week. It also lends itself to a simple comprehension exercise (after you have read through the poem several times with your child).

Answer these questions

What game does Ted play on **Monday**?   _____

Wednesday? _____

Friday?   _____

Choose from: shops, post, trains, police.

Simple stories, or passages from these stories, can be used for straightforward reading, to develop understanding by simple comprehension work, or to develop sentence construction skills through placing words in 'gaps', or in order.

Put the correct word in the space:

The gingerbread   ran away. man

and put the words in the correct order:

sun the is hot   the sun is hot

Try these

Read and put the correct word in the space:

> man, gingerbread, catch, run,
> can't, me, back, river

An old woman made a gingerbread man.
The gingerbread _____ ran away.
He said, 'Run, run as fast as you can,
You can't catch me, I'm the gingerbread man.'
He met a dog.
'Stop! Stop!' said the dog.
'No! No!' said the _____ man, 'You can't
    _____ me, I'm the gingerbread man'.
He met a horse.
'Stop! Stop!' said the horse.
'No! No!' said the gingerbread man,
'Run, _____, as fast as you can, you _____
    catch_____ , I'm the gingerbread man.'
He got to a river.
A fox came.
'Get on my back,' said the fox, 'and we can
    get across.'
The gingerbread man got on the fox's _____
    and they went over the _____ .
The fox sent the gingerbread man into the
    air, and ate him all up.

Jack and the Beanstalk

Jack sold his cow for some beans.
His Mother threw them in the garden.
In the morning a beanstalk had grown to the
    sky. Jack climbed up.
There was a castle at the top.
A giant was counting his money.
Jack ran off with his money.
He went down the beanstalk.
The giant came after him.
Jack cut down the beanstalk.
The giant fell down from the sky.
'The giant is dead,' said Jack.

Answer these questions

1. What does Jack sell?   _____
2. What grows up to the sky?   _____
3. What was at the top?   _____
4. Who was counting his money?   _____
5. What did Jack cut down?   _____
6. What happened to the giant?   _____

Choose from: a cow, a beanstalk, a castle, a giant, the
beanstalk, he died.

Only try these exercises when your child is reading quite well
(or at least they know phonic words well). Read through the
story with them, helping with difficult words.

5 Graded Word Searches and Crosswords

Use these games to improve your child's word knowledge.

Level 1

Find these words: bed, net, tap, cup, hat, cat, pot, pen, bat, ant, ten, egg.

```
b   e   d

a

t   a   p

        o

        t   e   n

                e   g   g

        h   a   t

        n

    c   a   t

    u

    p   e   n
```

Word search 1

Find these words: hot, mug, dog, mum, lip, fish, jam, leg, pup, man, pig, sun, run, red, tin, van, box, bus, dad, bag, six, zip, pen, fox, egg, big. (Word search is horizontal, left to right only.)

```
a  m  u  g  g  f  f  i  s  h  b  p
p  m  a  m  u  m  g  p  i  g  a  i
g  f  l  i  p  f  f  o  x  f  o  z
h  b  a  g  u  h  o  t  w  i  z  p
f  h  z  d  o  g  t  v  d  r  e  d
b  o  y  u  p  q  t  i  n  m  n  a
v  j  a  m  b  i  g  x  n  r  u  n
v  o  e  g  g  l  e  g  p  o  z  x
i  m  b  p  e  n  p  e  i  s  u  n
p  u  p  k  i  d  a  d  s  r  v  t
o  v  x  e  r  e  m  a  n  b  t  o
z  v  a  n  b  b  o  x  b  u  s  d
c  u  d  s  i  x  t  z  i  p  v  w
```

Get your child to write out the words as they find them, and to **say** them out loud.

Level 2

Find these words: fish, letter, shoe, duck, shop, tree, car, foot, bread, feet, book, ship, spoon.

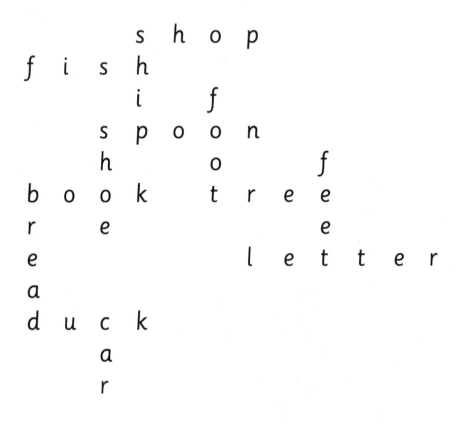

Word search 2

Find these words: fish, moon, bird, grass, sock, wood, door, house, light, frog, ball, hand, apple, ant, feet, kite, garden, queen, window, look, into. (Only left to right horizontally.)

```
a  c  g  f  m  o  o  n
g  m  r  f  i  s  h  b
f  e  e  t  b  a  l  l
d  o  o  r  b  i  r  d
p  p  n  h  o  u  s  e
l  w  o  o  d  e  m  x
e  o  k  g  r  a  s  s
s  o  c  k  f  r  o  g
f  l  i  g  h  t  a  n
b  a  l  h  a  n  d  o
a  n  g  a  r  d  e  n
o  a  p  p  l  e  i  o
k  l  o  o  i  n  t  o
a  n  t  k  i  t  e  k
q  u  e  e  n  d  c  a
i  u  b  l  o  o  k  f
t  w  i  n  d  o  w  g
```

Level 3

Find these words: old, back, new, apple, little, horn, there, over, down, three, born, added, out.

```
                              o   v   e   r
                      o       u
                      l   i   t   t   l   e
        a   d   d   e   d           h
        p       o               n   e   w
        p       w                   r
        l       n       t   h   r   e   e
        e                   o
                    b   o   r   n
                    a       n
                    c
                    k
```

Word search 3

Find these words: and, has, only, that, first, here, the, from, about, blue, was, her, brown, our, right, their, some, them, one, two, three, four, five, seven, eight, nine, want, well, went, were, what, when, where, which, who, will, you, your, more, much, most, must, morning. (Left to right, horizontally only.)

```
h  a  s  b  o  n  l  y  c  a  o  u  r
f  b  a  n  d  a  n  i  n  e  e  t  h
e  i  g  h  t  o  t  h  a  t  a  t  h
w  e  l  l  s  o  m  e  f  w  a  n  t
   f  i  r  s  t  u  w  h  e  r  e
w  e  n  t  h  e  x  z  h  e  r  e
t  h  e  m  o  o  w  e  r  e  t  g  m
   w  h  a  t  t  h  e  t  w  h  e  n
w  h  i  c  h  p  r  q  b  r  o  w  n
m  o  r  n  i  n  g  h  o  m  u  s  t
t  h  e  i  r  o  f  i  v  e  e  f  i
a  f  o  u  r  p  f  o  h  e  r  e  i
h  f  r  o  m  n  g  o  t  h  r  e  e
r  i  g  h  t  d  m  o  r  e  w  a  s
e  o  n  e  d  t  w  o  s  e  v  e  n
a  b  o  u  t  d  w  i  l  l  y  o  u
t  w  h  o  d  y  o  u  r  m  o  s  t
c  m  u  c  h  f  e  d  b  l  u  e
```

Level 4 – double blends and combinations

Find these words: blot, ship, clock, pram, spoon, moon, foot, feet, fish, clap, frock, sing, ring, rain, sock, spot, nest.

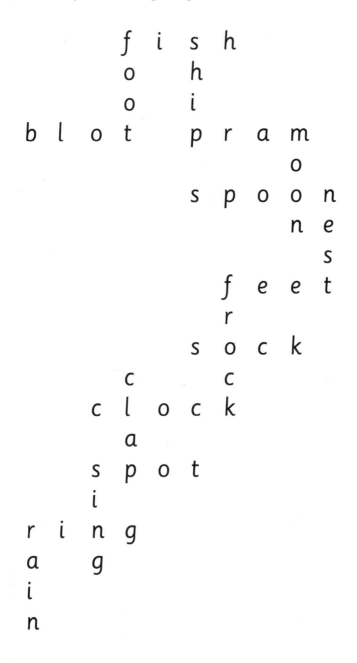

Word search 4

Find these words: black, chip, chop, chap, shop, shut, clap, clot, click, bring, cling, sting, clip, plan, plot, wing, frock, flat, flock, drop, drip, slip, slap, stop, stick, trip, trap, this, that. (Horizontally, left to right only.)

```
s  t  i  n  g  b  g  c  l  i  n  g  y  e  z
c  b  r  i  n  g  u  a  h  e  s  h  o  p  u
u  b  u  p  l  a  n  b  c  l  i  p  r  a  x
a  r  b  l  a  c  k  i  e  e  d  r  i  p  o
d  r  o  p  d  t  r  a  p  g  p  l  o  t  n
i  n  f  l  o  c  k  d  c  h  i  p  e  e  m
a  s  h  u  t  a  s  l  a  p  l  s  l  i  p
s  t  o  p  r  d  p  c  l  a  p  u  f  q
f  l  a  t  b  u  z  a  f  t  h  a  t  n  v
g  r  c  h  o  p  e  e  f  r  o  c  k  o  m
e  m  b  l  a  o  t  d  s  l  n  c  l  o  t
b  c  l  i  c  k  i  m  w  i  n  g  j  l  k
l     g  t  r  i  p  h  l  t  h  i  s  i  b
a  s  t  i  c  k  o  s  c  h  a  p  s  t  a
c  t  i  c  b  l  a  b  a  x  r  o  c  k  y
```

Level 5 – middles and endings

-ea-, -ou- and -ai- middles, with more -sh and -ck endings.

Crossword 1

Find these words: round, cloud, rain, train, tail, stairs, fish, dish, seat, clock, sock, kick, stick, sack, brick, drain.

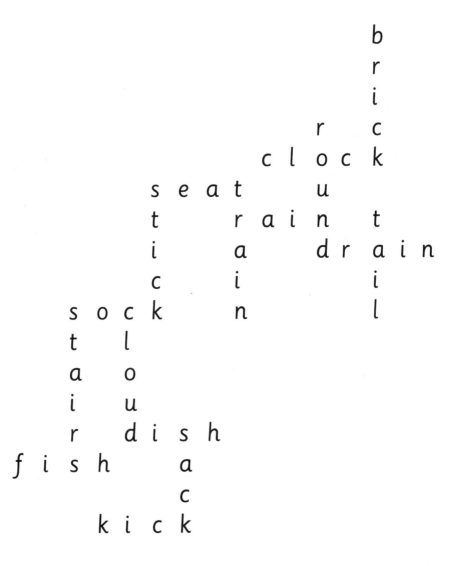

Word search 5

Find these words: sound, out, shout, ground, chain, fail, air, chair, fair, fairy, crash, dish, cash, wish, rush, brush, tea, dream, steal, read, heat, cheap, meat, fear, neck, lick, suck, sick, back, rock, knock, black, stuck. (Left to right, horizontally.)

```
m e s m e a t r a d n e s d a t w h
a s t e a l w a n f e a r n r o c k
g s t a t e a t e d e d d r e a mp
a c a s h i l p r a s t b r u s h o
n a i r i d i s h a i c r a s h q r
e o c l f a i l e n t s o s u c k r
b i s i c k r o f a i r y n e c k s
a c h e a p r a s s r u s h t h u t
a g r o u n d o o d l b u s t t i l
s i l b l a c k b r o c h a i n o b
i j o w i s h e e s k n o c k p o
h b a c k s s o u n d e t r i mo o
t h e s t i mo p n h e a t l i s l
t f a i r f l o x s r s t u c k s i
t a l n e c k c r a y z x s h o u t
p o o mi n t c h a i r s t r a n b
z o u t b r e e t s e d l i c k t i
y f f g r e a d s t e n b o z a i r
```

6 Reading Stories

The following series of stories and other reading matter are for reading **to** your child, and for reading by them. Word structure is based on work completed up to this point in the book, so most words should be fairly easy to read. 'Samantha' contains some awkward words, but with help and explanation of meaning it should be possible for your child to really enjoy the reading experience.

For more advanced learners, the following poem and questions will provide a good test:

Samantha

Samantha saved the world today
While she was going out to play
Down by the Village cricket ground
She found a Giant stamping around
On spying her, he gave a roar
And moved to crush her to the floor.
Samantha never raised a hair
Just fixed him with a steady stare
And in a second, in a wink
The Monstrous Giant began to shrink
Until when smaller than the hay
The tiny Giant ran away.

Much later, by St Stephen's wall
A wicked Witch was next to fall.
(She'd hired the pitch on easy terms
to turn the people into worms.)
Samantha never lost her cool

Just fixed an eye upon the ghoul
And in a trice the evil trog
Began to change into a frog.
New arms, new legs, fresh green skin tan
Off hopped the Witch-Amphibian.

At noon a Dragon passed that way.
He'd had a really jolly day.
He'd burnt the grass, ignited trees
And brought the whole town to its knees.
Samantha saw the park in flames:
'That's where I play my skipping games!'
Right in the middle of Main Street
She viewed the Beast with some slight heat.
A glance enough to fry a skate
And Dragon fast incinerate.

In Pacey's Pond a Thing from Space
Was threatening the Human Race.
(Much worse than that, I heard a scare
It might decide to settle there.)
Samantha, little heroine
Transfixed this nasty alien.
Before it cried, 'Exterminate!'
Or, 'Laser Earth!' it was too late.
She'd wiped the slate, erased the Blot,
Her eyes had vaporised the lot!

Into the Grounds of Haunted Hall
Samantha chased her bouncy ball.
There was a rustling of fear:

'Watch out! Watch out! Samantha's here!'
The Goblins, Ghosts, and Vampire teams
And every evil thing of dreams
From basement to the second floor,
Ran headlong through the open door,
Intent on one thing in their flight –
Escaping from Samantha's sight.

Approximately half-past three
Samantha skipped back home for tea.
'O, Mummy!' cried the tiny tot,
'Today I've done an awful lot.
I've rid the World of Nasty Things
Like Ogres and X-File Beings.
I'm sure that if I'd not been there
There'd be no Earth for us to share.'

Now Mummy'd had a frightful day
A head that wouldn't go away,
The vacuum cleaner bag had bust
And covered everywhere with dust.
So, to her shame she never heard
A single, solitary word,
And in an absent-minded way
Was prompted, wearily, to say:
'Don't talk whilst you are eating, there
And please, Samantha

Please

DON'T

STARE.'

Questions

Write the answers in sentences.

1. What happened to the Giant?
2. How did Samantha stop the Witch turning people into worms?
3. Why was Samantha cross with the Dragon?
4. What was in Pacey's Pond?
5. Why was there a 'rustling of fear' in Haunted Hall?
6. Why did Mummy take no notice of Samantha?

Wally Wimbush and the Others

'There is a bear at the bottom of the garden,' said Grandma.

Mary Melvin went to see.

In the tree house she found a small bear eating eggs, with his feet on the table.

'Hi, Kid,' said the bear.

'Who are you?' asked Mary.

The bear sat up.

'Wally Wimbush is my name, fighting witches is my game,' he said.

He switched on a TV near his head.

'Look,' he said, 'a witch has taken over your school.'

Mary looked. It was true.

'What can we do?' she asked.

'Stay cool, Kid,' said Wally, 'we can beat this thing.'

He took a black box from the table, and they went to the school.

'Evelina, the wicked witch, is your teacher,' said Wally.

In the class, the witch stood at the front.

'Okay,' she said, 'bring me your dinner money, and your jewels, or I will turn you into frogs and stamp on you.'

'This is a very, very nasty witch,' said Mary.

'Nasty, nasty,' said Wally.

They put their money and the black box on the table.

'This box is good,' said the witch, picking it up. 'What does it do?'

'It makes you go pretty,' said Wally.

Evelina smiled a wicked smile.

'Good, good,' she said. She pressed a button on the box and shot up in the air. She was stuck fast to the ceiling.

'Help! Help!' she cried. 'Let me down!'

'I think she looks good up there,' said Mary.

'Cool,' said Wally, 'she can sleep up there for ever.'

'Please, please let me down,' said the witch, 'and I'll be a good girl.'

'Okay, okay,' said Wally, 'Keep your hair on. Just press the button again.'

Evelina pressed the button and vanished in a puff of blue smoke.

'Where has she gone?' asked Mary.

'In the dark, dark wood,' said Wally, 'in a

dark, dark, smelly pond.'

'So, Evelina is sitting in the middle of the pond?' asked Mary.

'Yes, yes,' said Wally. 'We beat the witch this time.'

Mary went home. She was tired.

The next day she would ask about the black box, and about the dark, dark wood.

Brock the Robot

'I have an Army,' said Wally.

'How big is it?' asked Mary.

Wally counted in the air with a finger.

'One...Two...Three...' he said. 'Mother got a flea, put it in a teapot and made a cup of tea.'

'What has that to do with it?' asked Mary.

'Nothing,' said Wally, 'but it sounds good.'

He went to the door.

'Come with me,' he said.

Mary followed.

They went to a cave.

On the rock at the side it said: 'GO AWAY. I AM A MONSTER. I WILL EAT YOU.'

Wally stood, and shouted: 'Helloooooo!'

Mary hid by a tree.

Out of the cave came the smallest monster you ever saw.

'You're not a monster,' said Mary, 'just a teeny pipsqueak.'

The monster stamped his foot.

'I **am** a monster,' he shouted, in a tiny voice. He went back in the cave, and said it again: 'I **AM A MONSTER!**'

'That is why he lives in a cave,' said Mary, 'so that when he says things, it comes out loud.'

'Cool it, kid', said Wally, 'you've just upset him.'

They walked away from the cave.

'So, that is your army,' said Mary.

'There are some more to see,' said Wally, 'on another day.'

They passed a scarecrow.

Mary looked back.

'I think that scarecrow is following us,' she said.

Wally looked.

'It's Brock, the witch's robot,' he said.

They went up to the robot.

'You are Brock the robot,' said Wally.

'No, no,' said Brock, shaking his head, 'I am a scarecrow.'

'Scarecrows don't talk,' said Mary.

'I didn't talk,' said Brock.

'Yes, you did,' said Mary, 'I was just here, and you said something.'

'It was someone else,' said Brock, 'someone else said a word.'

'This is silly,' said Mary, crossly.

'See,' said Brock, 'you just said something.'

Wally poked a finger at the robot.

'What do you want?' he asked.

Brock's eyes opened wide. You could hear the little wheels in his head go round and round.

'I have come with this,' he said. He held up a small bag.

'What is it?' asked Mary.

Brock smiled a big smile.

'The witch gave me this invisible dust,' he said. 'I put it on your heads, and you vanish back to the witch's castle.'

Wally looked at him for a second.

'What about a Test?' he said.

'A Test, a Test? What is a Test?' asked Brock.

'Before you do something you must try it on yourself. That is a Test,' said Wally.

'I see,' said the robot. He opened the bag and sprinkled the dust on his head. He vanished in a puff of pink smoke.

'Bye, bye, Brock', said Wally.

'That must be the world's most stupid robot,' said Mary.

'I think so,' said Wally. He looked at his watch.

'I must go now. The Others come soon to bring me things to fight the witch with.'

Later, Mary lay down to sleep. One day she would find out who the Others were. But that was another day.

The Witch's Castle

'The Others gave me these,' said Wally, giving a small paper bag to Mary.

Mary looked.

'These are sweets,' she said, 'just sweets.'

'They must do something,' said Wally. 'The wicked witch has all the people from the town at the dark, dark castle.'

'What for?' asked Mary.

'She wants them to make her Boss of the town,' said Wally.

He picked up the bag of sweets. Then, they set off for the castle.

'You go across the big field, into the dark, dark wood and up to the witch's castle on the hill,' said Wally.

In the field, there was a big hole in the ground.

'Babbit, babbit,' said someone from the hole.

'It's Grilla,' said Wally. 'He thinks he is a rabbit.'

'But really, he is a gorilla,' said Mary.

Things today were getting very stupid.

From the hole came a small gorilla. Tied to his head were two big woollen ears.

'Babbit, babbit,' said Grilla.

'Rabbits don't say that,' said Mary.

'Babbits babbit all the time,' said Grilla, 'don't you know that?'

'You are even too big', said Mary. 'Rabbits are small.'

'Babbit, babbit,' said Grilla, taking no notice. 'I must find a big, fat carrot to munch.'

He went down the hole again.

'That gorilla should be in the jungle, or up a tree,' said Mary.

They walked on, into the dark, dark wood and on to the dark, dark castle.

The witch was talking to the people of the town.

'Now, now, you nice, pretty people,' she said. 'Make me your queen, and I will give you food and nice, nice pretty things, and you will not have to work.'

All the people cheered.

'Liar, liar, your coat's on fire,' said Wally.

He took the sweets and went up to Evelina, the wicked witch.

'Ooo, nice, nice, boy,' said the witch, 'you have got me some sweets.'

She looked in the bag.

'I like the smelly sweets best,' she said.

She took a black, stinky one, and popped it in her nasty, black mouth.

'Oooh, sicky, sicky,' said the witch, looking very happy.

Just then, smoke began to come out of her ears, her nose, and her black mouth.

'Okay,' she said to the people, 'I am going to tell you the truth. I don't like you people. I only like bats and slugs and nasty things. When you make me queen I am going to take all your money, and lock you up in jail.'

The people booed.

'Good sweets,' said Wally Wimbush. 'Now, the people hate the witch.'

They left the castle and went home.

Mary woke that night when it was still dark. She crept down to the tree house. Inside, the bear was talking to a little green man with an eye on the end of his nose.

'So that is an Other,' she said.

But what the Others were, and where they came from, she was not sure.

Wally Wimbush and the River

'Look,' said Wally, the next day, 'the witch has stopped the river.'

Mary looked at his TV. The water was not running along the river any more.

'We must save the town,' said Mary. 'No one can wash their socks.'

They went to the dark, dark wood.

In a tree was an elephant with boots on.

'Why are you up a tree?' asked Mary. 'Elephants don't go up trees.'

'I do,' said the elephant. 'Mice and ants tickle

my feet, and run up my trunk.'

'That's why they call him Jelly,' said Wally. 'He shakes if he sees a bee or a bug.'

Jelly came down and they went on to the witch's castle. By the castle, the witch had made the river into ice with a magic spell.

At the river stood Brock.

'I am a guard,' said Brock. 'No-one must pass me.'

Wally had a think for a second.

'Now', he said, 'if Jelly sits on you, you can't stop us, can you?'

Brock, the robot, had a think for a very, very long time.

'Come on,' said Wally, 'or it will soon be next week.'

'Okay,' said the robot, 'let the elephant sit on me, and you can pass by.'

So Jelly sat on Brock, and Mary and Wally went on to the river.

'What did the Others give you?' asked Mary.

'They gave me this,' said Wally. He held up a small match.

'I don't think that little thing will melt a river,' said Mary.

Wally dropped the match on the ice. There was a giant 'FIZZZZZ...' and a long crack began. It got bigger and bigger until the ice had gone.

'No more smelly socks,' said Wally, as the river

began again.

At night, red and green lights came down from the stars to visit Wally.

'Little green men from space come to bring him things,' said Mary. Those were the Others.

Now, she knew something about something. But what she knew, she was not sure.

Wally Wimbush and the Blobbers

'There's no more ice-cream in town,' said Mary Melvin.

'That is because Evelina, the wicked witch sent her nasty blob people to steal it all,' said Wally.

'What are blob people?' asked Mary.

'They live in the bottom of the dark, dark castle,' said Wally. 'They feed on ice-cream and grow as big as houses. Then the witch sends them out to squash all the people, and all the animals.'

'Bad, bad, nasty witch,' said Mary.

Wally showed Mary a very tiny pin.

'The Others gave me this,' said Wally. 'I can try it on the blobs.'

'Not very good, is it?' said Mary. 'A teeny, tiny pin to kill a giant blob!'

'I have one pin for all of you,' said Wally. 'One for me, one for you, one for Monster, one for Grilla and one for Jelly.'

'This is bad, very bad,' said Mary. 'I hope I

don't drop my little pin in the grass, just before a blob comes to squash me.'

'Stay cool, Kid,' said Wally. 'We will beat these blobbers.'

After dinner, they all met at the tree house. Wally Wimbush put a big cross on a map.

'This is me and my army,' he said. He put a small cross at the dark, dark castle. 'This is the witch and the blobs,' he said. 'The plan is for my army to surround the blobs.'

'How many blobs are there?' asked Mary.

'About a hundred,' said Wally. 'or even one million.'

'How can five of us with pins beat one million giant blobs?' asked Mary, crossly.

'Just wait and see,' said Wally.

They marched up to the castle. The wicked witch stood on the castle top, and sent the blobs after Wally Wimbush and his army.

'Squash the silly bear,' she shouted, 'and make me Queen of the world!'

Mary held her little pin as a giant blob came after her.

'Help!' she cried, 'A great, black blob is going to squash me!'

Then the little pin shot out of her hand and into the blob. Green sticky stuff came out of the blob, and it grew smaller and smaller, until it was just a tiny blob in the grass.

The teeny blob ran away.

All over the field the blobs were turning into teeny blobs. In the end, they had all vanished.

'Hooray!' shouted Wally Wimbush and his army.

Back home, Mary told Grandma about Wally Wimbush and the wicked witch.

Grandma shook her head.

'No good will ever come of it,' she said. 'When did a small bear ever beat a wicked, wicked witch?'

Mary Melvin said nothing. She had found that small bears can do much more than you think.

Wally and the Witch's Train

'Brock, the robot, is making a railway line round the town,' said Wally Wimbush.

They went to see.

'What is it for?' asked Mary.

'It's for a train,' said Brock. 'A train runs on a railway line.'

'I know that,' said Mary. 'I knew that from when I was very small.'

'Don't ask then,' said Brock.

Soon, the railway line was finished. It had little stations where you got tickets. There was Happy Station, Smiley Station, and Stinky Station. Soon, there were children in a line waiting for a train at all three stations.

'It's not like Evelina, the wicked witch, to help children,' said Mary. 'What is she up to?'

'Bad things,' said Wally. 'The Others gave me this.'

He showed Mary a big, red balloon.

'A balloon!' said Mary. 'A balloon! How can that save the children from the witch's castle?'

'Just wait,' said Wally. 'It will do something important.'

Mary didn't think so. Balloons were not good things to beat witches with.

Later, the witch came down the railway, riding on a small train.

'Look, Kidneys,' she said to the children. 'I am a train driver! Come for a nice trip, you sweet little things!'

'She will lock them up in her castle to work until the world ends,' said Wally Wimbush.

The witch went to the Stations, picking up all the children.

'On this balloon it says, "Give to a witch, then blow hard",' said Wally. 'Quick, take it to her and give it as a present.'

Mary took the big, red balloon and handed it to Evelina.

'Very good, little girl,' said the witch. 'I can see that you know that I am the Queen.'

Then, Mary Melvin blew on the balloon.

That did it! The balloon, with the witch still

holding it, shot up in the air, and began to float into the clouds.

'Help! You stupid girl!' screamed the witch, turning purple in the face. 'Just wait till I get down there. I'll scramble you for my dinner!'

She floated away until she was a very small dot, far, far away.

'That is the first time I ever saw a witch fly,' said Wally Wimbush.

'If she keeps on going,' said Mary, 'she may get to the moon.'

'Then it is a very bad day for the moon men,' said Wally.

For the children, it was a good day. Wally made Brock give free rides around the track until it was dark.

'Soon, the wicked witch will be back,' said Mary to herself. 'By then, Wally, his army and the Others will be ready.'

Wally Wimbush and the Sleepy Music

One morning, Mary Melvin woke up to hear music. She went to see Wally Wimbush in the tree house.

'What is the music?' she asked.

'ZZZZZZZ,' said Wally, fast asleep.

Mary went to the big field. In Grilla's burrow it was the same: 'ZZZZZZZ,' said Grilla.

At Monster's Cave, there was a bigger sound.

'ZZZZZZZZZZZ,' said Monster in the cave.

In the dark, dark wood, Jelly was asleep in the biggest tree: 'ZZZZZZZ,' said Jelly, the elephant.

Mary went back to the tree house. On Wally's TV, she saw the witch sitting at the castle. She had her biggest smile on her face. By her side was a small radio playing music.

'Magic music!' said Mary. 'It put all the people to sleep.'

On Wally's table was a small packet with brown powder in it. On the front, it said:

'Throw in the air, and let the wind blow it at the witch.'

'Powder from the Others,' said Mary.

She took it, and threw it into the wind.

Up in the sky, a small, black cloud blew across to the witch. Then, it began to rain... but, it only rained on the witch. The drops of rain were big, as big as plates. Soon, the witch was so wet, she look like a fish. Slowly she sank into the mud at her feet until it was up to her neck.

'Grrroooo,' said the wicked witch.

The music stopped.

Wally Wimbush gave a long yawn, and woke up.

'Hi, Kid,' he said. 'What's up?'

'The witch put you all to sleep,' said Mary, 'but your powder made it rain on the witch. She is stuck in the mud.'

'Good, good,' said Wally, 'leave her for one million years. Now go away for a long time. Someone important is coming for tea.'

'Is it the Queen?' asked Mary.

'More important than that,' said Wally. 'The Others are coming for cream buns and peanut butter.'

Mary went back to the house. She wanted to know why the sleepy spell did not work on her.

'I remember,' she said. 'Grandma gave me one of her sticky ginger sweets at bed-time.'

'Eat it,' said Grandma, 'real ginger is good for you.'

So, ginger sweets may beat the spell of the wicked witch.

'Yuk!' said Mary. 'I hate ginger sweets, even if they are good for you.'